The Door to Fruitfulness

When God Invites Us to Bear First Fruits

Tammy L. Jordan

THE DOOR TO FRUITFULNESS
When God Invites Us to Bear First Fruits

By Tammy L. Jordan
Copyright @ 2011 ShadeTree Publishing, LLC
Print ISBN: 978-1-937331-16-0
e-Book ISBN: 978-1-937331-17-7
Cover art by Linda Minigh
Foreword by Dr. Rick Metrick

Scripture quotations marked "KJV" are taken from the King James Version. The KJV is public domain in the United States.

All rights reserved. This book is protected by copyright. No part of this book may be reproduced or transmitted in any form or by any means, electronic or mechanical, including photocopying, recording, or by any information storage and retrieval system, without permission in writing from the publisher.

The purpose of this book is to educate and enlighten. This book is sold with the understanding that the author and publisher are not engaged in rendering counseling, albeit it professional or lay, to the reader or anyone else. The author and publisher shall have neither liability nor responsibility to any person or entity with respect to any loss or damage caused, or alleged to have been caused, directly or indirectly, by the information contained in this book. The information in this book does not necessarily reflect the opinion of the publisher.

Visit our Web site at www.ShadeTreePublishing.com

*To my parents
who taught me that all things
are indeed possible with God!*

Foreword

By Dr. Rick Metrick

Honour the Lord with thy substance, and with the firstfruits of all thine increase.
                    -Proverbs 3:9 KJV

When Tammy Jordan told me that she was going to write a book on how to bring glory and honor to the Lord, it was all I could do to contain myself. As the founder of Just Honor God, Inc., I hold the practical side of honoring God near to my heart. I would be hard-pressed to think of someone whose life is more devoted to honoring God than Tammy. Her life of giving and serving is a beautiful reflection of the God she loves and honors.

The Door to Fruitfulness was written for those who desire to produce more for the Lord, but find themselves inundated with unproductive busyness. Tammy makes a clear distinction between bearing regular fruit and bearing *First Fruits*. She reminds us that we can live an honorable life, one that honors God through *First Fruits*.

Each chapter in this book reminds us that *First Fruits* is an invitation to every believer from a patient and compassionate God who longs to make us more productive for His Kingdom.

My prayer is that this message will reach people like you, who desire to honor God with their *First Fruits*. So, grab yourself a cup of hot tea, sink into your favorite chair, and enter through the door of fruitfulness.

Table of Contents

Introduction 1
Giving Our Heart for Salvation 5
Giving God the Freedom to Prune Our Life 9
Giving More Productively 13
Giving Our Praise and Worship 19
Giving Our Time 23
Giving Our Talents and Gifts 27
Giving Our Labor for the Harvest 31
Giving Our Resources 35
Giving Our Compassion 39
Giving Our Abundance 43
Giving Our Today 47
Giving Our Future 51
Giving Our Best 55
Giving Our Life 59
Giving With Purpose 63
Giving Our Legacy 67
First Fruits Prayer 71
About the Author 74
Fruits of Labor, Inc. Training & Retreat Center 76
About the First Fruit Series 79

I waited patiently for the LORD; and he inclined unto me, and heard my cry. He brought me up also out of a horrible pit, out of the miry clay, and set my feet upon a rock, and established my goings. And he hath put a new song in my mouth, even praise unto our God: many shall see it, and fear, and shall trust in the LORD.

-Psalms 40:1-3 KJV

Introduction

Honour the Lord with thy substance, and with the firstfruits of all thine increase.
-Proverbs 3:9 KJV

When I considered how to bring glory and honor to the Lord, Proverbs 3:9 came to mind. At first, it seemed so straightforward, and I assumed that it had a singular meaning; namely, if we want to honor the Lord, then we would simply offer the *First Fruits* of our finances.

As I continued to ponder the verse, a second thought came to mind: why would God wish for us to honor Him with just our financial resources? It seems unlikely that our Lord, who created Heaven as an extravagant place that we cannot truly comprehend, would just request our material substance to give Him honor.

After persistent meditation on this verse, several other considerations came to mind. Our "substance" is not limited to material wealth, nor is our "increase". God asks for the substance, which is our very life. He also requests all, not just part, of what causes us to increase. "Increase" takes several forms such as salvation, talents, or financial resources. We must understand how different increases in our life allow us to produce fruit for Christ.

Following salvation, our first attempt at producing fruit generally occurs in our own vineyard where we harvest our good deeds and services that we provide for others. However, this fruit isn't *First Fruit*.

Once we are producing fruit, we arrive at a place where God invites us to bear *First Fruits*. Here at this open door of invitation, where we sit on the cold stone of our own uninspired works, we see the gentle and loving hand of Jesus ready to lift us from our miry pit of good (but fleshly) efforts of fruit bearing, so that He may establish our Godly goings as He desires.

As we pass through the Door of Fruitfulness, we leave the comfort of our grove, and enter God's Vineyard, where we are to *be* the vine, not tend a vine. Here we allow ourselves to be pruned, nourished, and fertilized by God. The result of this step into a deeper faith walk with God is *First Fruits*.

The process of bearing *First Fruits* does not happen overnight. It is our human nature to question God just as a child would question a parent. More often than not, we spend too much time in fruitless actions and bearing hindering attitudes that cause us to miscarry the harvest God desires from our life.

When we set our heart towards God and become willing to allow His hands to shape us, He will guide our steps to bring forth *First Fruits*. He is patient with our questions and with our fear of complete faith and reliance on Him. It is a learning process for us. Through His continuous molding, He refines our life as we yield to Him season after season.

This book is a map to the Door of Fruitfulness. It is a journey from our vineyard to that of the Master Gardener. It provides a new perspective of how we can offer Him the *First Fruits* of our substance and of our increases in order to give Him an abundance of honor that He desires and deserves.

Tammy L. Jordan

First Fruits Truth

Without salvation, we can never enter into God's Vineyard.

Giving Our Heart for Salvation

Honoring the Lord with our *First Fruits* starts by personally accepting His gift of salvation. Giving anything to God, without first having a relationship with Him, is simply a human effort to appease Him.

Due to the sinful condition of man, we are separated from God by a great gulf so wide that no amount of human effort can cross it. God is holy and righteous. We as mankind have nothing to offer to Him in our own righteousness, because there is nothing righteous outside of God.

> *As it is written, There is none righteous, no, not one:*
> -Romans 3:10 KJV

All the good things and works we count as most precious and valuable here on earth, God sees as nothing.

> *But we are all as an unclean thing, and all our righteousnesses are as filthy rags; and we all do fade as a leaf; and our iniquities, like the wind, have taken us away.*
> -Isaiah 64:6 KJV

Despite man's filthiness, God sent His only begotten Son to die on a cross as eternal atonement for our sins, thus providing us with His gift of salvation. It is in that saving grace, we find that our life, hope, and future are secure in the blood of Christ. He no longer is just God; He is our Father.

> *For as many as are led by the Spirit of God, they are the sons of God. For ye have not received the spirit of bondage again to fear; but ye have received the Spirit of adoption, whereby we cry, Abba, Father. The Spirit itself beareth witness with our spirit, that we are the children of God: And if children, then heirs; heirs of God, and joint-heirs with Christ; if so be that we suffer with him, that we may be also glorified together.*
> —Romans 8:14-17 KJV

As our Father, God desires the best for our lives. He wants to prosper us in ways we know not of, but first we have to give our heart to Him. Once we lay aside our pride and accept Him as our Father, we are then able to honor Him by offering our heart and thanks as *First Fruits*.

Fruitless Actions and Thoughts Toward God:

God, I am afraid of Your salvation. I fear that by accepting it, I will embark on a road I don't want to travel, and my life as I know it will cease to exist. I contemplate my ability verses Your ability to outline the plans for my future. How can I have faith that You will always love me, even when I fail? How do I know You desire the best for me?

God's Fruit-Producing Response:

Come, My beloved. My yoke is far easier than the path of your own hands. It's a road not without hardships and troubles, but it will be a life of My peace, a place where My grace is sufficient to endure any path you are facing in life. Your faith is secure in My salvation, and I will always be your Father. Fear not, because you will always be My child. Rest your heart in My deliverance from sin.

My First Fruits Offering:

God I do not fully understand Your free gift of salvation, but I do understand that it is a path that I yearn to follow. Today, I offer my heart and thanks as the *First Fruits* of my salvation.

Additional First Fruit Thoughts:

_____

_____

_____

_____

_____

_____

First Fruits Truth

Without pruning, we cannot experience the new growth God desires for us.

Giving God the Freedom to Prune Our Life

Every Christian is called to bear fruit because we abide in the Vine of Christ.

> *I am the true vine, and my Father is the husbandman. Every branch in me that beareth not fruit he taketh away: and every branch that beareth fruit, he purgeth it, that it may bring forth more fruit....Abide in me, and I in you. As the branch cannot bear fruit of itself, except it abide in the vine; no more can ye, except ye abide in me. I am the vine, ye are the branches: He that abideth in me, and I in him, the same bringeth forth much fruit: for without me ye can do nothing.*
> -John 15: 1-2, 4-5 KJV

We must first understand how to bear fruit in Christ before we can live a fruitful life. Bearing fruit is a life-long cycle of allowing God to work in our life. In a vineyard, the plants are continuously prepared to yield fruit. Once harvest passes, the vines are immediately readied to yield fruit again for the next season. Our daily walk with our Father is similar.

Once we are grafted into the Vine of Christ, our Father lovingly attends to our branches. Because some parts of us may be damaged due to sin or hurts, He compassionately removes the dead areas. As we grow, He carefully lifts us from the ground and develops for us a support system of His unconditional love. We rest in His trellis of trust and our branches lengthen. In time, we yield a small harvest, after which, the loving Vinedresser prunes us for the next season so that we may continue to grow in productivity.

Fruitless Actions and Thoughts Toward God:

Savior, I understand that You are the vine, and I love the nourishment I receive from being a branch in You. But Lord, I'm just not strong enough to bear fruit. You would be better served by another more mature branch in Your Vineyard. I just want to enjoy the nourishment and security of Your Vine. To be honest Father, I've watched Your pruning methods in other's lives, and it appears unfair at times. Your life-shaping techniques seem too hard to endure. And God, what if I let You prune things in my life and then I still fail to produce any fruit? What then, Lord? What would I have to show for all my sacrifices?

God's Fruit-Producing Response:

My child, I see the greater plan for your life. I remove and restore with a heavenly vision, not an earthy view. Give Me your branches to prune. In the cutting away of the damaged and useless parts of your life, I will cause growth to flourish in you. In addition, as your roots delve deeper into My ways, you will find previously untapped resources. Trust Me. I have your best at heart.

My First Fruits Offering:

Father, I know that You see beyond today, and despite the discomfort, I'm willing to give You my life, so that I may see new growth. Today, I offer my life to You for pruning, so that I may bear better and more plentiful *First Fruits*.

Additional First Fruit Thoughts:

_____
_____
_____
_____
_____
_____

First Fruits Truth

Without accepting God's plan for productivity, we cannot sustain in our own strength without exhaustion.

Giving More Productively

Most often, we attempt to give more productively to God by increasing production. However, this concept is quite the opposite of what giving more productively actually means. The door of giving more productively is not entered by climbing through the window of additional spiritual activities to the point of physical and emotional drain. God does not call us to produce to the point of burnout, but rather produce in a sustainable manner.

Becoming productive is more than just producing more. Let's use a vineyard as an example to explain the point. We can increase productivity of the operation by two methods:
1. Increase the number of vines (i.e., increase the number crops by increasing the number of acres that are in production)
2. Increase the efficiency (i.e., decrease the amount of time it takes to harvest, or the amount of space required per plant)

Producing more fruit for Christ can be accomplished by doing more (taking on new roles and responsibilities) or by becoming more efficient (doing things with less time and effort). Many times, God may present opportunities for us to expand our labors. For example, we can start a prayer group, a leadership class, or a ministry to reach the community. However, being more productive overall is not something that we can do on our own. It is something that God does through us.

A comparison to the difference between simply producing more and being more productive is a question all sustainable farmers answer at some point in their growing career. There comes a point in time that a farmer may exhaust his available acreage or his time to manage more food plots.

A resourceful producer reviews what is most productive: how he can take the same space, use the most productive types of plants, and invest the same amount of time tending the plants to be more fruitful.

At some point as children of God, we run out of time, energy, and extra resources, yet, we still aspire to produce more for God. Our first inclination, to quench this desire is to pick up new projects, new missions, new callings, and add them to the list of things we are already doing for God. While these are good and Godly projects, they're not what God intended for our branch to bear.

At that point, we often find ourselves having several new projects that only weigh down our hearts and overextend our time even more. Eventually, we fail to complete any of the tasks, start to suffer from the overload, and question why God requires effort to the point of exhaustion.

Instead, the Father waits patiently to teach us the valuable lesson of tending His Vineyard. He deeply desires that we become entrenched in His gratifying methods of productivity. God wants us to give more productively, and this is something only He can make happen in our life. We must cry out for Him to make this change instead of us trying to produce more on our own with devastating results. When we enter through the doorway to His Vineyard, we willingly take on the role of the plant, and God assumes the role of our loving Gardener.

As our Caretaker, God needs complete freedom to work in our lives, even when we don't understand His ways. He enriches our soil with proper nutrients and provides water at just the right time. Sometimes we may feel like we are wilting and don't understand why He permits this. We cannot see that by withholding a little water, He is allowing our roots of faith to plunge deep into His grace, so that we can be sustained even through the worst droughts. As we start to grow more, He comes with sheers and begins to prune our branch of things that dramatically weaken our ability to produce more. Although this process may be painful, to be highly productive for Christ we must undergo extensive pruning. He is constantly walking past us and inspecting our leaves (heart) for disease (sin), because He knows that a trace of sin will eventually spread in time and destroy the entire plant.

After the pruning and the summer drought, we sometimes question whether becoming more productive was even worth it. But then the day comes for our harvest, and our loving Caretaker asks that we lift up our eyes to see the fruit produced from all of His efforts in our life. In disbelief, tears stream down our face when we see the magnitude of what God has accomplished and of the fruit that has come from our life, once He had freedom to tend to us as needed. In that moment, we embrace the concept of how to give more productively.

> *That ye might walk worthy of the Lord unto all pleasing, being fruitful in every good work, and increasing in the knowledge of God;*
> —Colossians 1:10 KJV

Fruitless Actions and Thoughts Toward God:

God I know what I need to do for You! I have a million thoughts, plans, and dreams ready to go. Honestly, I'm just waiting for You to give me additional resources and the strength to make these things happen. Now that I have finally experienced what it is like to bear fruit, I am ready to see the bigger picture of doing more for you. Though honestly Lord, sometimes I am bit exhausted about the busyness of the labors. I even feel my heart getting a little resentful at times, because I'm doing so much more, but I have yet to see the real results of my extra effort. Some days I just wonder whether it is really worth it at all...are You hearing me? Do You see my hands at work? When will the harvest that I've worked so hard to produce for You come to me?

God's Fruit-Producing Response:

Ah, My child, the one desire I have is that you rest in My timing and in the ways that I work, and not tell Me how to work. What I can do with a dollar, you cannot do with even a million dollars. What I can do in the twinkling of an eye, you cannot complete in a lifetime. You scurry around as if to prove you are a Christian, full of service, and yet I want you to stop trying to prove to others what you can do, and just be still and wait to hear My direction for your life.

I crave the day you are devoted enough to Me that you quit designing plans of service and start letting Me selectively use your energy, passion, and labor to produce far greater results in the spiritual realm. Your imagination wants to accomplish spiritual matters with a course of action designed by an earthly mind.

You must embrace the concept that when you rest in Me fully, the fruit of your labor will only come in My time, in My way, and for My glory. Fruitfulness was never designed for a mere stamp of approval from man.

My First Fruits Offering:

Lord, I desire more than where I am in my walk with You, but I have bankrupted my resources trying to walk after You in my own way. Lord, empty out this weary vessel, and exchange my good works for productive labors by working through me. Today, I offer all my plans, dreams, and aspiration to You, Father, so that You may demonstrate in me a healthy lifestyle of bearing *First Fruits* for Your Kingdom.

Tammy L. Jordan

Additional First Fruit Thoughts:

_____

_____

_____

_____

_____

Giving Our Praise and Worship

God created beings that surround His throne in Heaven, for the singular purpose to give Him perfect and continual honor, praise, and worship. Why then would He create in mankind the need and desire to return praise and worship to Him? It is remarkable that a sovereign God would find imperfect praise and worship appealing. Yet, all through the Bible, we are encouraged to praise, to give glory, and to honor God, not for the sake of others hearing you, but purely to worship Him.

> *Give unto the LORD the glory due unto his name; worship the LORD in the beauty of holiness.*
> —Psalms 29:2 KJV

When we imagine ourselves in God's position as our Father, we can clearly see the difference. For example, a parent may suggest to her child to reach out to another child that is clearly being excluded from an activity. There is joy when the child follows the specific instructions. However, a parent gets far greater joy when the child reaches out, of his own accord, and includes the other child. The same concept is true for God.

God does have other means of hearing and receiving praise and worship from beings that are directed to offer this up continually. However, He finds it far more precious when His children (without being asked) come and lift up their voices, shed a tear of joy in the dark, bend a knee, or raise a hand to honor and glorify His name.

What a beautiful picture we see when Christians unashamedly praise the Father. Our God is great, He is worthy, and our Heavenly Father needs to be honored. Our imperfect ways of worship and our prayers of praise are sweet music to His ears. As our Father, He treasures the tears that flow freely down our face when His joy moves our heart. It is in these moments that God rejoices in us being His child. This is fruit that comes from praising and worshiping the Great Almighty. He is delighted when we are happy and when we chose to express the fullness of our salvation to others.

However, the truest exaltation and most sincere adoration is when we lift up our voices in songs of praise in the darkest night, celebrating Him through tears of brokenness for His steadfastness, lifting hands in reverence through our worst trials of faith, confirming He is still our great Redeemer, and when we fall before Him to thank Him for knowing exactly what we need. This is when we give our *First Fruits* of praise and worship! He desires the deepest wellspring of our hearts and not just the rejoicing of our soul only when we are happy.

THE DOOR TO FRUITFULNESS

Fruitless Actions and Thoughts Toward God:

Times are wonderful right now in my life, and I'm so full Lord. My cup is just running over with Your sweet blessings. Lord, You have supplied my needs and the desires of my heart. I can't praise You enough for Your unmerited favor.

I find in time Lord, that my praise of Your goodness isn't as strong in the storms. In fact, Lord, I wonder whether You have left me alone to die in a desert place. My lips are closed, my hands are no longer high and lifted, and my heart has all but fainted. Lord, do You really expect me to offer praise to You and to sing in times of adversity? Is using my limited energy for tribute and song even possible, when my thoughts are saturated with how to endure this long, dark night? Surely, You cannot need this type of broken song and the painful lamenting of my soul. Lord, there is just nothing for me to give to You in the sorrow of my difficulties, but one day I will sing again in times of joy.

God's Fruit-Producing Response:

Precious one, I love to hear your praise and songs in exciting times. I'm glad that you stop to remember to thank Me for My gifts in your life. Yes, your voice in song is music to My ear as I find pleasure in your happiness.

It is not until your difficult midnight hour, that I hear what delights My soul. My ears listen for a broken song, a faint praise of survival, a weeping of your spirit that says, "Yes, You are my Lord, and I will continue onward in Your strength alone, because my strength is all but gone." When the fairness of the human voice is lost, I hear the pure beauty of your heart's song. It moves Me, as your Father, to rush in and bring you new life, to revive your spirit, to encourage your heart, and to lift the burden of your soul. I can move as a mighty wind to provide an immediate sanctuary in this time of storm. By entering the door of praise in your brokenness, your spirit is all that sang to Me. This type of worship is what I desire. Never fail to praise Me in your weakness, in your sorrow, in your depression and in the depth of your despair. Praise Me in your storm.

My First Fruits Offering:

Father, forgive me for only desiring to glorify Your name when all is well. May I receive a fresh filling of Your Spirit, so that I may lift up my voice even in a time of sorrow. Today, I offer the sincere, unedited song of my heart as the *First Fruits* of my worship and praise, regardless of any hardship I am currently facing.

Additional First Fruit Thoughts:

_____

_____

_____

_____

_____

_____

Giving Our Time

Time is such a valuable resource, and yet we waste it on things with no lasting value. We often wait, until we are on our last waking breath of the night, to pray and think about God. Sadly, God lives on this shred of time from us, many times for years or at least until our next overwhelming struggle. Patiently though, He continues to encourage us to spend more time with Him. It is usually in a period of despair that we grow close to Him, so much so, that we cling to every moment spent together. When our anguish passes, we usually slip back into our routine of spending scraps of time with God at the end of a long day. Our prayers are mostly out of duty and comprise thoughtless, repetitive words strung together. Somehow, this one-sided conversation is supposed to be meaningful, because our eyes are closed and our head is bowed.

What our Heavenly Father is waiting for is a real dialogue, intimate communion with Him, as our best friend and constant unfailing companion. When we start making plans to give the best of our time, a wonderful thing happens: we discover a rich and rewarding relationship. It is no longer a sacrifice of time, but a retreat where we gain a place of sanctuary in a hectic life.

> *As the hart panteth after the water brooks, so panteth my soul after thee, O God.*
> -Psalms 42:1 KJV

Once we recognize the peace in our life due to conversing with God, there is excitement over the next meeting and conversation, so much so, there are days we commune without ceasing. God invites us beyond the door of leftover time spent with Him, and welcomes us to a place of ongoing communication, where our relationship flourishes. When we reach the point of longing to be with our Father, just to talk, listen, and request nothing of Him, we are giving the *First Fruits* of our time.

Fruitless Actions and Thoughts Toward God:

God, my life is filled with activities. I am rushing just to survive each day. I have no extra time, even for myself. Surely, You understand that Sunday morning is the only time I can visit with You, and even then, I sometimes run late, because a fellow church member was driving under the speed limit. Entering into Your house, I am generally flustered and even angry. But thankfully, You understand that I am human.

Your Word encourages me to come to You with needs, but my actions often depict that I believe I have You on standby, hovering and waiting on my cry. Certainly, some of the problems I have caused myself, and I knew better before stepping into a sinful trap. However, I believe You will help me out, because I am Your child, and You love me.

I appreciate all the time You give to me in my hour of need. If more hours could be added to each day, I would have opportunities to actually talk to You instead of just having to cry out my list of requests.

God's Fruit-Producing Response:

Precious child, you have much to learn. Time with Me should not be allotted, as if scheduled like an appointment. Time with Me should always be desired. I am endlessly by your side. You rush silently through life, often painfully stressed, and I'm there beside you to offer communion, strength, wisdom, and guidance. You brush Me off as if I'm a weight, and yet in your struggles, you cling to Me as a life preserver. How do you ever think this relationship will grow if you only come to Me when you need something from My storehouse of blessings?

I long to hear you say, "Father, tell me a story about life, show me a direction I need to take, place me where You need me to be so I can be of service to You. My heart's desire is full devotion to the labors of Your plan for my life."

Please, slow down, wait on Me to speak, learn to hear My voice, commune with Me daily, and I will lovingly guide you. Then, you will understand that by giving your time to Me, I expand it exponentially.

My First Fruits Offering:

Precious Savior, remind me that all things are Yours. I am Yours, and my time here on earth is Yours. Help me to release my clasp on this very moment, and to place my future into Your loving care. Today, I offer You complete direction over my time as evidence of the *First Fruits* of a more deeply committed relationship with You.

Additional First Fruit Thoughts:

_____
_____
_____
_____
_____
_____
_____

Giving Our Talents and Gifts

It is commonly believed that only certain people have a talent. While it is true, not everyone has been gifted with a beautiful angelic voice or fingers that glide over piano keys to make a sweet melodious sound, we each have a talent or gift that we can use for God and the furtherance of His Kingdom.

Talents and gifts come in every form, and we are not to worry about being the best at our talent, rather, we are called to give our best effort to glorify God. You may realize that your knack is preparing meals for shut-ins or those suffering from illness in your church. It could be that working with children, college students, or seniors is what you enjoy. Others may be gifted in bringing comfort to ones that are hurting.

Because we are the body of Christ, we each have different abilities, which when combined, function together as a complete unit.

So we, being many, are one body in Christ, and every one members one of another.
 -Romans 12:5 KJV

If we could all preach, then who would sing? If we could all sing, but had no teachers, then who would teach? If we could all teach, but had no dedicated prayer warriors, then who would pray alongside of us in difficult times?

If we all had the same skill, there would be incompleteness in the body of Christ. There is no ability too small or insignificant for God's work. The Father is patiently waiting for us to take our own natural gifts, seek His face and guidance, and dedicate these capabilities for use, specifically to magnify His name and honor Him by giving the *First Fruits* of our talents.

Fruitless Actions and Thoughts Toward God:

God, there are so many others far more accomplished and have more experience working in Your Vineyard. Lord, I sit in the pew with clasped hands and a silent voice, because You really don't need me to give of my limited abilities. I continue to justify my actions with the excuse: not everyone has a calling in the talent department. So Lord, I am content to come to Your house and remain unchanged, still seated outside the door of fruitful service.

God's Fruit-Producing Response:

Draw close, My beloved child, and allow Me show you how true talents and gifts are used for My Kingdom. Talent is not in the skill, as much as in the giving spirit. You must look diligently for ways to serve. Let Me teach you to see others' needs as I see them. In that view of the world, I will reveal how you may be of assistance. When you allow Me to combine all your efforts with other fellow laborers, it is a remarkable sight to behold. Don't fear the changes I make in your life, because those adjustments foster growth. Allow Me to freely move you out of your normal comfort zone. In that movement, you will find the passion that I have prepared just for you. It is imperative to not bury your life in the world of "I can't". Instead, give Me sway over your future, and I will create a new and wonderful opportunity of "You can, through Me". Sharing this newly embraced zeal with others will become joy in your life!

My First Fruits Offering:

Lord, I humbly pray for You to inspire me to use the gifts that You have planted deep within my being. Allow me to realize these previously untapped resources, unselfishly and without hesitation. May I not value these talents for my own glory, but for Your glory. Today, I offer my talents and gifts, regardless of the value I place on them, as the *First Fruits* of my increased faith that God is able to create much out of limited abilities, if only I maintain a willing attitude of service.

Additional First Fruit Thoughts:

_____
_____
_____
_____
_____

Giving Our Labor for the Harvest

While resting at our Father's table we enjoy envisioning our inheritance in Heaven as joint heirs with Christ and reigning with Him for an eternity. At the time of our personal salvation, we are adopted into a heavenly family as sons and daughters of God. We treasure claiming Christ as our friend, the One who would lay His life down, shed His blood, and rise again. Through these acts, He accomplished our salvation at the cross.

In times of trouble, we eagerly claim Him as our source of refuge. At a point of bitter unrest, we call upon Him to claim His source of peace. We dine at His spiritual buffet of blessings and feast on His word, while forgetting we are called to be servants.

God did not have to save the world by using the hands and voices of humans to proclaim the gospel. He could have found other ways to reach a lost and dying world. Instead, He chose to use His children as instruments to point others to the source of eternal life. Once we accept the gift of His salvation, He invites us beyond the comfort of the spiritual dining room and out into the fields of humanity, to labor for

His Kingdom. We are to bear His name and His light to guide to the cross those who are lost in the darkness of sin.

> ...Lift up your eyes, and look on the fields; for they are white already to harvest.
> -John 4:35 KJV

Many of us only wish to glean the benefits of feasting at His table. Labor seems to be a foreign thought in today's Christianity; and sadly, this is a time that the need to harvest souls is the greatest. God directs us to be His hands and feet. We are also called to give the best of our labor. We should be willing to commit dedicated efforts and premium energy. This is when God receives the *First Fruit* of our labor for the harvest.

Fruitless Actions and Thoughts Toward God:

We are sons and daughters of the King. I delight in the thought that I have a place of value. Fellowshipping with others in the body of Christ is what it is all about. We enjoy each other and appreciate the benefits of coming to the house of God. Drinking and feasting from Your word at church is all that I need. It is nice to come in, sit down, and find sanctuary for my weary soul. Lord I'm confused because You promise me rest, but then You lead me to labor.

God's Fruit-Producing Response:

Oh my sons and daughters, please open your eyes! I know you need a safe place to come and renew your spirits, but you are to take that refreshed energy outside the church to a world that is perishing. You must learn to have compassion for those wounded by a life a sin, and be willing to humble your spirit to do whatever you are called to do in that moment of time, regardless of how menial the task. It is needful that you rise up to labor in My Vineyard. Many Christians delight in the fellowshipping of the saints. Few laborers want to reap what was previously sown. Godly companionship is for your betterment, to strengthen you, so that you have an increased desire to reach out to the unsaved. It is not merely to increase your social circle. Go! Linger no longer inside the comfortable walls of the church, but rather run to the fields prepared for reaping, as the season of harvest is short.

My First Fruits Offering:

Father, I am here. Use me and send me. I will wait patiently on Your gently bidding and will move at Your slightest suggestion. No longer Lord, will I stand with hands folded, waiting for others to attend to my needs. Strengthen me and give me a servant's heart. I need to learn to see through the perspective of Your eyes, so I might be the first to respond to Your tasks in the vast field of humanity. Today, I give up my comfortable seat at Your table to go into the fields to work as the *First Fruits* of labor for the harvest. I understand that You need my personal efforts to win souls for You.

Additional First Fruit Thoughts:

_____
_____
_____
_____
_____

Giving Our Resources

When giving to God, we generally think only of contributing monetarily. Ministry certainly requires money. We understand that as a Christian, we have a responsibility to give back a portion of our resources for the specific purpose of furthering the dispersion of the gospel. Thankfully, God does not require us to give to Him to gain salvation. He simply gives us His best gift free of charge. In addition, our Savior does not command that we give a certain dollar amount each year, thereby possibly excluding those in poverty. He does, however, ask that whatever we do give, we give cheerfully.

> *Every man according as he purposeth in his heart, so let him give; not grudgingly, or of necessity: for God loveth a cheerful giver.*
> -2 Corinthians 9:7 KJV

If we desire to bring Him honor in our giving, it must not be what is leftover, but rather what is first. We are called to give the *First Fruits* of our increases, not a residual portion. Sadly, many sons and daughters of God place no importance on contributing anything monetarily to God's work, or they bestow gifts with strings attached, believing they have the right to dictate how every penny is used, instead of allowing God to handle the matter.

Even more grievous to God, we fail to understand that resources are not just financial. Donations of our resources may include giving more time, compassion, wisdom, or understanding. When we comprehend that our increases are not just financial, but include anything that God has blessed us with, we are able to start giving the *First Fruits* of all our resources.

Fruitless Actions and Thoughts Toward God:

Lord, I toss in a few dollars into the offering plate every Sunday. In the Bible, You fed the multitude with only a boy's lunch. I know You can do amazing things with little, so would You miss my small gift? Psalms 50:10 says that You already own the cattle on a thousand hills.

Others in Your congregation have far more than I do, and just waste it. Why don't You press more on their hearts to contribute out of their abundance?

Honestly, I struggle to understand why You need all of my resources in addition to my finances. I have a very good plan for my life and my assets, Lord. I give some to You and also find a way to still enjoy the material increases that I've labored for each week. How do I know the church will responsibly use my hard-earned money and precious time?

God's Fruit-Producing Response:

I am limited as your God due to the lack of faith you place in Me to provide. You worry about giving Me all of your resources, and continue to live in fear that I will strip you of life's necessities. Your tight grasp on life causes Me to withhold the many blessings I long to pour into your life. You are My child, and I desire to give good things to you. Even more heartbreaking, you often contribute with a resentful heart, or bestow gifts only for the unimportant praise of man. Every resource you have is already Mine. I just wait patiently for the day that You place every possession into the care of My faithful hands. In that moment, you will see what can be done with all that you hold dear.

My First Fruits Offering:

Redeemer of my soul, I desire to relinquish all my resources to Your care. Empty my hands of things that I have no need of, and fill them with Your desired supply, so that I may better serve You. Today, I offer all my substance as the *First Fruits* of my resources and place trust in Your abilities to supply all my needs.

Additional First Fruit Thoughts:

_____

_____

_____

_____

_____

Giving Our Compassion

The Good Samaritan comes to mind when thinking of bestowing kindness upon another. Compassion for the lost, the forgotten, the broken, the wounded, and the undeserving, many times at our own expense, is what Christians are called to share with the world and with fellow brothers and sisters in Christ.

Compassion is the fruit of love. Love is the greatest of faith, hope, and charity; therefore, we quickly understand that freely giving compassion to others is one of the greatest of the *First Fruits* we can offer to God.

The fruit of compassion has the ability to take the shape of many different forms. We see in the case of the Good Samaritan, he offered physical care and monetary provisions to help the wounded stranger. A similar example in today's world would be stopping for someone who had wrecked. We could be a Good Samaritan for the day, and freely give our assistance. We must pausing and ask ourselves do we readily pass by the ones wounded in heart and spirit, or even worse, by those people hurt by our own words or actions. Would we daily step over their brokenness, while ignoring the pain they are experiencing? It is not easy to ask God to open our eyes to people's needs, so that we may tend to those bruised by unseen injuries of life.

While it is often easier to show compassion to our loved ones, it can actually be harder to do when they have hurt our feelings, like those close to us can so easily do. We must have the courage to go a step farther and ask God to reveal the hurts that we have personally caused to others, be it our spouse, our children, a church member, our pastor, or our dearest friend.

We cannot ignore castaways in need of the compassion of Christ either. If we started having compassion on the less fortunate, the drug addict, the fatherless, the homeless, the dying, and the lonely just imagine how many lives would be touched by Christ. Many devoted Christians will shy away from giving compassion to those outside their circle thinking that duty is another's calling.

The hardest people to grant compassion to are those who lied about us, destroyed our marriage, abandoned our friendship, stole from us, or humiliated us by publicly poking fun at our faith. When extending compassion to these people, we offer the best of the *First Fruits* of compassion.

> *Ye have heard that it hath been said, Thou shalt love thy neighbour, and hate thine enemy. But I say unto you, Love your enemies, bless them that curse you, do good to them that hate you, and pray for them which despitefully use you, and persecute you:*
> -Matthew 5:43-44 KJV

THE DOOR TO FRUITFULNESS

This type of self-sacrificing love is the *First Fruits* of God's authentic love flowing through us.

Fruitless Actions and Thoughts Toward God:

God it is easy for me to have compassion for those who love me. I'll even go a step farther and help those in need, maybe even offer help to those who have caused their own wounds. God, I simply don't understand the concept of loving my enemy. It's unnatural. Am I really able to help my enemy by loving them? An enemy has abused me, and worse yet, may have even abused Your name in the process. Lord, do you really expect me to love my enemy and those who will use my tenderheartedness against me? The world tells me that this is an unhealthy way to live.

God's Fruit-Producing Response:

My dear child, you are called to love all, and yes, all means all. There is not a fine line between love and hate, as the world defines love and hate, but rather a great gulf fixed between the beauty of true, selfless love and bitter, destructive hate. I desire the best path for your life. Anger towards an enemy will take root in your heart and soon grow into bitterness thus preventing Me from using you.

When you love your enemy, it is in this moment that My love shines through you. It does not mean you are to be a doormat, but rather a light that stands as a beacon in a world filled with revenge. All those who wish to cause you harm will only see the image of Me in your life. Through these wonderful acts of compassion, you may be the very tool I use to lead your worst enemy to My saving grace.

My First Fruits Offering:

Restorer of my life, pour into me Your compassion at any cost. Lord, may I be able to reach out and love deeply those who have betrayed me. Today, I offer my compassion to everyone who needs it despite the circumstances as the *First Fruits* of compassion.

Additional First Fruit Thoughts:

_____
_____
_____
_____
_____
_____

Giving Our Abundance

All we have to do is look around to see how blessed we are in life. God has showered our lives with His unending mercy and grace. We not only have a full cup, but one that has been pressed down, shaken together, and running over.

> *Give, and it shall be given unto you; good measure, pressed down, and shaken together, and running over, shall men give into your bosom. For with the same measure that ye mete withal it shall be measured to you again.*
> —Luke 6:38 KJV

Gladly, we accept all of the exciting and unexpected blessings of abundance that pour into our lives. Sadly, we often don't do anything with it. It is not until we consider the bounty God has entrusted us with and offer it to Him, that we understand fully the *First Fruits* of giving an offering out of our abundance.

At this point, in our Christian service, we know how to present a tithe to God. As His children, we learn to respond to His request of sacrifice, out of love and not because of duty. Our desire to show gratitude for all Christ relinquished as the Prince of Heaven, just to save us, is a principle that serves us well. It reveals a Godly perspective and encourages us to not be greedy with possessions. Giving an extra offering, especially something as precious as extra time, is a treasure that He greatly enjoys receiving.

Fruitless Actions and Thoughts Toward God:

Lord, I've learned how to tithe, and I even do so when there is little to give. I've not really meditated on the principle of presenting an offering. However, I must admit that concept seems an extreme action for this day and time. Let me review this whole process: You bless me with abundance above and beyond my needs, I return a portion to You, and then You want me to donate even more? Lord, I'm just not sure about the reality or the benefits of this whole process.

God's Fruit-Producing Response:

You cannot out give Me. When I press on your heart to contribute beyond the normal tithe, just do as I request. I desire to magnify you in unimaginable ways. Do not bestow upon Me gifts from a selfish heart banking on what you will receive in return, but give because I have blessed you enough to be able to give in times of limited finance, as well as times of abundance.

Wait on Me, and be prepared to give what I ask. Do not spend precious energy in worry about recovering that which you just gave.

All in due time, you will start to understand the process of bearing My fruit. Then in the darkness of your night when you have a need, I will impress upon hearts of others to give of their abundance to meet your most urgent need. In those hours, you will appreciate the importance of quick action when I beckon you. It will ignite a new passion in your heart to contribute, not only when the storm passes, but also while facing obstacles. Sometimes the most beautiful offerings you give are dispensed in the middle of your own distress.

Give as I request you to give. Question not the results, or what I will do with your offering. Just lay it on the altar and go your way. I will take care of the rest.

My First Fruits Offering:

Comforter of my spirit, pour into me wisdom to offer You all that is asked of me. May I be willing to release my life into Your hands so that I gain a deep abiding relationship with You, Lord. Today, I offer the abundance of my life into Your care as the *First Fruits* of my belief in Your abilities to care for me in ways that I can't comprehend.

Additional First Fruit Thoughts:

_____
_____
_____
_____
_____
_____

First Fruits Truth

Without us giving our today, God cannot effectively change our tomorrow.

Giving Our Today

Often as Christians, we find that somewhere along the journey, we start to slow down and rest in the activities we used to do for Christ (i.e., previously teaching Sunday school, working with the youth, leading the choir, or studying the Bible). We are content to live in the past, because that is where our service is located. Proudly, we recall our earlier devotion to Christ's work, as if that exempts us from the present. Somewhere along the way, we decided that we have contributed enough time for God and that we should take a break.

The same God that gave us the ability to toil in the fields of humanity for Him in the past, is the same God that asks us to give the *First Fruits* today. He calls to us many times in a still small voice, "Will you serve Me today? Will you lift up your eyes to see, even now, the fields are white for harvest?"

> *Therefore said he unto them, The harvest truly is great, but the labourers are few: pray ye therefore the Lord of the harvest, that he would send forth labourers into his harvest.*

-Luke 10:2 KJV

We need to stop looking back at the past long enough to understand that yesterday is finished and all we have is the here and now.

God's requests of service often seem unreasonable. We have excluded Him from our present life so much that He no longer fits. We have to rearrange our schedules to accommodate His work in our life and quench the thought that His request of extra effort seems unfair and too demanding from a loving God. He waits longingly until we desire to see Him come once again and gather the *First Fruits* of our today.

Fruitless Actions and Thoughts Toward God:

God, I'm weary as my life is very hectic trying just to live with all the commitments. Fitting service to You into my life right now is a daunting task. Most of my time is devoted to family. I have served You for many years, and I rejoice greatly in the times that You have worked through my life in the past. I've even experienced Your revival in my heart from time to time, and what an exciting fire I felt turning to serve You. I've accomplished the dreams of yesterday; and today, I just want to reflect on those joyous times and live in memories. Everyone deserves a season of rest, and You know intimately the pressures I have in my world. I'm content knowing that I've accomplished some really great things for You, and those labors must count for something.

God's Fruit-Producing Response:

Beloved, I do not count your past offerings of fruit as present-day credits. You are called to serve, to give, and to harvest until you are called home to live eternally with Me. As My servant, you are needed to labor in My Vineyard daily. When you replace service for Me with pleasures or unnecessary labors of this world, you are missing the blessings that you once received in the past. Miserable, empty, and always seeking for something more, you travel through this time wondering what is absent from your life.

It is not until you return to Me and begin giving your energy and time towards the ministry I have prepared for you, that I can bless you in amazing ways. Currently, My blessings of today's harvest are withheld, because they are delivered during your service, not while you are resting in past harvests.

My First Fruits Offering:

Father of Light, I long to serve You now more than ever before. Let me not get caught up in yesterday, but rather be perched and ready to seize all opportunities You have waiting for me this day. For my *First Fruits* of today, I freely offer my hands to be used at Your discretion.

Additional First Fruit Thoughts:

_____
_____
_____
_____
_____

Giving Our Future

Take therefore no thought for the morrow: for the morrow shall take thought for the things of itself...
—Matthew 6:34 KJV

While we are not to live in tomorrow, because tomorrow may not come, we can allow God to prepare us to give Him the best of our future.

By keeping our heart open to God's leading, even when we don't understand, we allow Him to work freely and to equip and strengthen us for what is yet to come.

By allowing the Father to tenderly prune our branch today, we will notice an overall increase in spiritual health, and through this act, we will be better prepared for next season.

When we do not allow our Father to correct and nourish our current situation, we miss out on our future harvests.

Fruitless Actions and Thoughts Toward God:

Lord, I feel like I'm under Your constant supervision. From my viewpoint You are continually changing, adding, removing, and tending to my life. Sometimes, I act as though I have everything covered for the moment and have no need of Your assistance. Most of the time, I feel this way when I am attempting to hide sin from You.

I know You have my best at heart, but there are periods of time, I don't want to be prepared for a future harvest, because being productive takes so much effort and growth on my part, that I'm not sure that is the direction I want to go today.

God's Fruit-Producing Response:

My child, remember what I said in Jeremiah 29:11: I know the thoughts I think toward you - thoughts to give you a future and a hope.

The work in your life is ongoing whether you wish to grow or not. Sometimes that labor is towards recovery from self-inflicted damage, and at other times, it is as intended a preparation for the future. My greatest yearning is for you to live in the moment of today, while allowing Me to freely prepare you for tomorrow.

I need to have complete access to your heart, so that we may have fellowship that is uninterrupted by the depleting effects of sin. In this time of intimate companionship, I am able to encourage you to take new directions. This change in the course of life will open doors to new contacts, whom are needed for future projects.

Never fear the purpose of My tending to your life. My ultimate goal is for you to be nourished completely by My love, so future harvests are fulfilling and productive.

My First Fruits Offering:

Father, please help me embrace You in such a way that my desire is just to move forward even if there is sacrifice involved. Please, let Your labor in my life be for growth purposes, and not endlessly due to sin damage. May the future harvest not be delayed, due to my wandering away from Your heavenly vision. Today, I offer all that I am, in this moment, for you to shape and direct my life as the *First Fruits* of my future.

Additional First Fruit Thoughts:

_____

_____

_____

_____

_____

_____

First Fruits Truth

Without giving our best to God, we cannot experience His full vision for our life.

Giving Our Best

Raising fields of produce and flowers as a business has converted a quaint hobby garden into a micromanaged operation to produce the best, blemish-free crop possible.

Each year as I gather the harvest, my hands come across the best of the best. It may be the tomato that is giant and perfectly shaped, the pepper that takes two hands to hold, the pumpkin that is ten pounds larger than all the rest, or the fresh berries that are so plump and large that even I'm amazed. Most people assume those would be the portion of the harvest sold quickly, because it would command a higher price. Not so in my case, these special products are joyfully packaged for our family and friends. They are the first fruits of an earthly harvest.

> *All the best of the oil, and all the best of the wine, and of the wheat, the firstfruits of them which they shall offer unto the LORD, them have I given thee.*
>
> -Numbers 18:12 KJV

For Israel, God also desired the actual physical harvest as an offering. Spiritually speaking, God wants the best of our life's harvest too. He requests that we give Him our best to further His purpose and Kingdom.

Fruitless Actions and Thoughts Toward God:

Father, I understand that You long for the very best of my life. Lord, I don't understand why You expect me to offer the best things in my life to You after You have already given them to me. If You allow my labors to produce these results, should I not be able to keep and enjoy the very best of it?

God's Fruit-Producing Response:

My child, giving the best of your harvest is a very easy principle to learn, but quite difficult to practice. When you give Me the best of your *First Fruits* I hold the most sacred parts of your life in My hands, a place where nothing that can destroy, harm, or steal them. As you grow and mature, you will understand that when you freely offer your best to Me, I will come and pour out My abundance upon you. Your blessings will be far beyond the earthly realm you currently live and work. I don't promise that it will be returned in the same form as what you are giving, but instead, exactly what you need. I will create in you a life that you could not have hoped for without Me. You will be living out My vision for your life, and that will only produce great and mighty outcomes for My glory.

My First Fruits Offering:

My Heavenly Counselor, minister to me so that I may understand that my best is what You desire. Help me to overcome my selfish tendencies, so that I can joyfully put my best in Your secure hands. Today, I offer my very best *First Fruits* to You.

Additional First Fruit Thoughts:

_____

_____

_____

_____

_____

_____

First Fruits Truth

Without giving our life fully to God, we cannot experience the joy and peace that come with a surrendered life.

Giving Our Life

The giving of our life to Christ is summed up by one word: *surrender*. Such a negative word in our vocabulary, yet such a beautiful word in Christ. For it is when we die to ourselves and abandon our life for the sake of Christ, we save it. For the very first time, we truly live.

Surrender troubles even mature believers to the very core. A season of relinquishment of our ways is draining, and yet when it passes, we find a great sense of peace.

As we walk more closely to our heavenly Father, we find He asks more of us to surrender to His care. At first, it may start with a surrender to study His Word more. A challenge may be issued to our hearts to pray more. These examples are simply a yielding of time, devoting more of who we are to the One in whom we place our trust.

> *Trust in the LORD with all thine heart; and lean not unto thine own understanding.*
> —Proverbs 3:5 KJV

A calling from God requires a journey of surrender that is rarely easy. The greater the calling, the greater the submission. Amazingly though, surrender is optional. However, refusing to yield to God, separates us from His path for our life.

God asks us to abandon our way of life. Even though He intimately knows the priceless results of our complete surrender, He does not demand it. Instead, He patiently urges our heart to release the things we cherish the most. In our complete and total surrender, we find peace even in the midst of a season of extreme pruning.

Fruitless Actions and Thoughts Toward God:

Lord, strangely, I'm happy to leave my eternity in your hands, but I want to remain in control of the details on earth. You created me with free will, and God, I am happy to seek Your opinion for big things, but I cannot see why I need to turn every single aspect over to You.

Lord, You keep coming in the still small voice saying You want my life. How does giving it to You save it? You gave us a mind, should we not be responsible to plan our own life? I certainly cannot understand how dying to myself actually makes me live? It seems to contradict everything.

In the past, I've submitted to some pruning in my life, and may I be completely honest with You Lord - it was not pleasant. So, I wish to quickly remove myself from that process whenever I want. Please understand, I'm good with the way my branches look. Maybe I'm not as productive as I could be, but I'm content.

God's Fruit-Producing Response

Oh My precious, precious child if only you would fully trust that I know far better than you what you need in your life. My perspective is heavenly. Your perspective is at best, a short window of your current situation tainted by past failures.

Pruning does feel harsh and unfair at times, but you withdraw your life from My hands before I am able to complete the process and show you the beautiful results of surrender. When you rest all that you have in Me, I can move swiftly and freely. Doors will open and close quickly, and you will be prepared in body, mind, and spirit to spring into motion at the exact time I need you to move. When you surrender only in part, I come up against the wall of your will and have no place to maneuver until your will is released. As a result of your choices, you feel like you often live in dark and trying times.

Your fear and lack of trust keep you from laying everything down and allowing Me to have opportunity to transition you. In a season of complete surrender, I will sort through your life with loving hands, keep things that are needed and remove things that are weights, even when they seem important. After the burdens are removed, you will have room for Me to start the replacement process. I will guide your steps to the new path. When fear stops you again, you live longer in the land of want. Follow My steps through the obscure season of surrender, and I will lead you to the dawning of a new and glorious day!

My First Fruits Offering:

I simply desire to be Yours, Lord. Help me to surrender all that I am each day to allow Your hands to create something beautiful from my life. Today, I offer my life on the altar of sacrifice as the *First Fruits*.

Additional First Fruit Thoughts:

_____
_____
_____
_____
_____
_____

Giving With Purpose

Our abilities are summarized by the word *competency*. We often aspire for that word to describe our life, but when describing our Christian walk, it can actually decrease our faith. We may ask ourselves the questions: Should we not strive daily to be self-sufficient, accomplished, and capable of handling future decisions? Are these not good and positive traits of being competent, and do these qualities not allow us to give more effectively and with a polished purpose? Why is being proficient a negative attribute for our spiritual relationship with Him? Still bewildered of how competency can diminish our faith, I waited for the still small voice to enter into the conversations of my heart.

When we dismiss the idea of human competency from our spiritual journey, we turn away from the idea of what we can do *for* God and embrace something far greater. We adopt the idea of what God can do *through* us. What we can accomplish *for* God is always limited by our fleshly nature (fears, fretting, and sheer lack of ability). What God can do *through* our surrendered lives is untold. We face nothing impossible, no obstacle too great, no vision too large, nor fear too crippling. These outcomes occur because we die to self and surrender everything that He has asked us to place in His care. Now, we are His hands and feet. God's flawless handiwork moves uninhibited through our life. We are united as one, an extension of our Father, Savior, and Friend. Our limited competency proves unnecessary, because by His strength, a greater work is perfected in us. We no longer have to do things for God with *our* ability alone, but rest in *His* ability to move through us, and accomplish a more fulfilling purpose for our life.

> *I can do all things through Christ which strengtheneth me."*
> -Philippians 4:13 KJV

This learned mannerism, to rest in Him, translates into giving with a greater purpose. We give with His purpose.

Fruitless Actions and Thoughts Toward God:

I know You are God Jehovah, the Great Almighty, my Refuge, Hope, Salvation, and Strength. You have given me abilities and strengths to be used for Your Kingdom, but why, when I strive to use my abilities for You, do I not feel fulfilled in the accomplishments? These are good labors toward heavenly things, but many times I feel exhausted rather than excited, more consumed than renewed, and unfocused instead of filled with purpose. Lord, what is missing? I feel depleted to a greater extent, as I accomplish more for You, as the need to achieve greater future things intensifies after previous goals are met.

God's Fruit-Producing Response:

These questions will lead you to rest your abilities in Me. I see your labors, and while they are honorable and respectful, they are still flowing forth from your strength and not Mine. I cannot help you do *all* things in your strength alone.

When you pour yourself into a series of projects that are stamped with the approval of your own accomplishment, the more drained and exhausted you will become, even when they are spiritual ventures. Other than the momentary delight of seeing a goal attained, there's little, to no lasting joy or sense of fulfillment.

It encourages My heart that you have reached this point of desiring to be filled with My vision for your life. You are now entering the stage of finding true, sustaining purpose. This dream is not going to come from your own hands. I may extract from your life passions and use your natural abilities, but your future direction involves Me working through you. Your life will become a channel in which I operate, and I need to have you fully devoted to My mission in your life. Once you lay aside the desire to quench the human need to produce for mere accomplishment's sake, I can reach out My hands and work through yours. The purpose I lay before you appears to be a far greater cost than most are willing to pay, but in the end, more rewarding than anything your hands have previously touched. In allowing Me to work through you, the only thing this world will see coming from your labors is your faith in Me. All other efforts have no ability to replenish the soul as My purpose does in your life.

My First Fruits Offering:

Lord, I desire to submit to Your calling and purpose for my life. I know it may look very different from my plans, but I'm willing to step out by faith and seek after You with my whole heart. Your purpose, revealed through me, will be far greater than my ability to labor with fleshly hands alone. Through this transition, I'll have joy and fulfilment. Today, I surrender the *First Fruits* of giving with purpose.

Additional First Fruit Thoughts:

_____
_____
_____
_____
_____
_____

Giving Our Legacy

At some point as Christians, we find ourselves thinking about our legacy. There have been a number of songs written about the idea of what type of legacy we will leave for those who follow us. More importantly, are we walking a good path for someone else to follow behind us?

When the word legacy is mentioned, immediately, the thought of children come to mind. We contemplate how are lives will be remembered in the next generation. Will our career efforts be important twenty years from now? Will our philosophies and ideas matter in the future? Will loved ones remember us for the good accomplished? Some people may think they have no legacy. I must submit that everyone has a legacy; however, the question is – *is it memorable?*

Instead of getting so caught up with what people will remember us for, we must first consider what God remembers about our legacy, whether He'll use our example in life for future generations. We often forget, the Bible is full of everyday people who left a legacy that God is still using today.

> *By faith Abraham, when he was called to go out into a place which he should after receive for an inheritance, obeyed; and he went out, not knowing whither he went. By faith he sojourned in the land of promise, as in a strange country, dwelling in tabernacles with Isaac and Jacob, the heirs with him of the same promise: For he looked for a city which hath foundations, whose builder and maker is God.*
>
> -Hebrews 11:8-10 KJV

With an ordinary life by our standards, what should we do to leave a legacy that God can use to speak to generations to come? The best place to seek after a life filled with extraordinary fruitfulness is to ask God to use us endlessly. Once we pray for His direction, we must follow at whatever cost, challenge, or fear. The results will be a Godly, fruitful heritage. As long as we have breath, it is never too late to leave a rich, full legacy.

What type of legacy will we leave? Will it be one of soul winning? Love? Compassion? Kindness? *First Fruits*? Will we retire a worn, note-filled, tear-stained Bible? Will we live surrendered to His call on our life so that others may see Him in us? Will we leave a faith so strong that it is the very essence of all that we are in life? Will we die to ourselves to find that it is through Him that we live? Will we leave a legacy that simply honors our Lord and Savior?

Fruitless Actions and Thoughts Toward God:

God I often wonder whether anyone is actually watching my life. Will my choices affect that many people? As I slip and fall into temptation, will it

THE DOOR TO FRUITFULNESS

really matter that much? When I do not surrender my life to You, does it really harm those around me? My laboring, purely to accomplish good works for Your sake, still achieves honorable results on this earth. Is embracing Your purpose for my life that important to create a future legacy for others to remember?

I serve You and do love You, Lord, but I just cannot see far enough ahead have a good concept of how You are working in and through my life, to draw others to You.

God's Fruit-Producing Response:

All labors you do today, My dear child, frame new foundations for those to follow after you. Your efforts are building upon foundations already laid by believers that walked before you. Please take hold of the idea that you live in a world of past, present, and future laborers. What you do today prepares the way for greater plans in the future. When you decide to leave My work undone, the burden of neglect must be carried and overcome by those who walk beside of you or who follow after you.

My child, strive to leave an honorable memory of your life. Seek after My ways and allow My loving hands to create, today a legacy for those who will come after you. They will be thankful of your preparations for their journey, just like when King David gathered all the building supplies so King Solomon, his son, could build the Temple. Leave the legacy of giving, but most of all, leave a devoted faith, a pure love of all things spiritual, and a life of seeking My will for all your days.

My First Fruits Offering:

Alpha and Omega, the Beginning and the End, Your legacy always has been and always will be. My legacy, Lord, in the scope of Yours is a vanishing vapor, and yet, You still treasure it. Please Father, fill me in such a way that my steps are pure and pleasing to You and to all that encounter me on this short journey, called life. Today, I offer my legacy as the *First Fruits* of a life lived for You. May it hold a rich Godly, heritage due to Your endless refining efforts.

Additional First Fruit Thoughts:

_____

_____

_____

_____

_____

_____

First Fruits Prayer

Honour the Lord with thy substance, and with the first-fruits of all thine increases.
                                        -Proverbs 3:9 KJV

Lord, because of Your work on the cross at Calvary, I know that You deserve praise. I understand that You also desire honor through the *First Fruits* of all my increase, but Lord, I daily fail to give my all to You.

Sometimes I must admit that bearing spiritual fruit for a coming Kingdom is not top on my priority list for the day. Rather, most of my time is spent trying to build an earthy empire by withholding labor, resources, and offerings from You, in order to grow in my direction.

Father, I struggle with managing my time to have enough energy left in me, to rise above an apathetic lifestyle, towards Your service and release my greatest resource of time to Your watchful care.

Of the many opportunities I have to use my talents and return praise unto You, I sit silently in the pew praying that someone else will rise up in my place. Please, help me to be the one who moves at

Your first nudging, and to get out of my comfort zone of indifference. I want to be where You need me in Your church, meeting the needs of Your body.

Lord, I choose to be an instrument of compassion. May I cover people with Your love not my own shallow concept of human love, but Your rich everlasting, selfless love. Infuse me with a love that heals even the heart of my worst enemy, and by their healing I will find joy.

My dear and loving Savior, I desire the rich harvest of today, tomorrow, and to give my best to You, with only Your purpose and goals in mind. I submit my life to Your tending and pruning, and surrender my plan for Your will.

I rest in You, not only my life on earth and my promise of a future in heaven, but also the legacy I'm leaving for all that follow after me. My prayer dear Lord is that when people see my life, they no longer see my image, but only Your great reflection. I want to freely offer You the *First Fruits* of my entire being - body, mind, soul, and spirit. The whispered prayer of surrender that I offer up to You is simply, "Use me as You see fit."

Additional First Fruit Prayers:

About the Author

Growing up in the beautiful, lush mountains of West Virginia, **Tammy L. Jordan** has always had a deep love for nature. At the age of five, she dreamed of owning a farm, and that desire only grew with time. After many years of working in agricultural research, Tammy stepped out by faith and went full time with her company Fruits of Labor, Inc., which marries agriculture with culinary arts. The company expanded into retreat-style ministry with the purchase of the 218-acre Fruits of Labor Training & Retreat Center.

The Retreat Center offers women's retreats, special interest day retreats, and the Training Center is scheduled to offer a new culinary and agricultural program for recovering addicts beginning the summer of 2013. Tammy's next books *The Seed Sower* and *Seeds of Recovery* are slated to be released Fall 2013. Please visit www.fruitsoflaborinc.com to learn more about retreat opportunities and training programs. Tammy's desire to become more fruitful for God has become her priority in life.

Author's Acknowledgements

To my Lord and Savior: Who knows the passions within my heart and also knows how to allow them to be used for His glory.

To my family: Who never fail to amaze me with their endless love and support.

To Dr. Rick Metrick: Who encouraged me to, "Just do this!"

To my church family: Who have nurtured and loved me since birth.

To ShadeTree Publishing: Who believed in the book, worked diligently to make this publication possible, and helped me grow in the process!

And finally, to my dearest friend: Who has seen the very depths of my soul and still loves all of me. The one who knows the song of my heart, and who will sing it back to me when seasons of storms threaten to steal my peace.

Fruits of Labor, Inc. Training & Retreat Center

Fruits of Labor is where the fruit of the earth meets the fruit of the Spirit. The training and retreat center is designed as a place of sustainability in agricultural practices, lifestyle principles, and spiritual growth for longevity of service.

Come experience a setting where agricultural research, culinary passion, and hospitality coincide with training programs and renewal retreats.

Fruits of Labor is dedicated to providing a mountaintop experience that prepares individuals with education, experience, and training in agriculture, culinary, and hospitality industries. At

Fruits of Labor, we grow much of our own fruits and vegetables used to prepare mouth-watering meals for retreat guests seeking to rejuvenate and draw away from the hectic pace of their spiritual ministries.

The retreat center, situated on 218 acres of land at over 3200 feet in elevation, will surround the mind, body, and spirit with a peaceful, natural environment. Walking trails, gardens, and other recreational activities are available. The retreat center offers serene accommodations with private meditation areas and beautiful vistas to enhance the experience.

Types of Training and Retreats:
- Pastor/Pastor Couples Retreats ~ Come, and allow God to renew, restore, heal, and re-energize your ministries. We have scholarship opportunities available for pastors.
- Restoration Retreats ~ Various retreats are available throughout the year to help strengthen the church body and family. Healthy churches, first start with healthy individual Christians who are motivated to pray, serve, and labor.
- Leadership Retreats ~ Leadership retreats help individuals and groups draw away from the normal hectic pace of life, find time to relax, and let their mind open to new ideas and concepts.
- Culinary and Agricultural Training Program ~ This training program is specially designed for recovering addicts. The program works with the whole person, and offers training in the culinary industry and farm-to-table movement to help increase job opportunities.

To learn more about *Fruits of Labor*, schedule a retreat, or make a donation towards one of the programs, please contact Tammy Jordan at fruitsoflaborinc@hotmail.com or visit our website at www.fruitsoflaborinc.com.

About the First Fruit Series

The *First Fruit Series* is designed to bring honor to the Lord and is based upon the principles found in Proverbs 3:9.

Honour the Lord with thy substance, and with the firstfruits of all thine increase.

(KJV)

Bearing First Fruits is a unique and wonderful part of the Christian experience that grows out of surrendering our will to God's will for our life. The key ingredient to bearing First Fruits is to set our heart towards God and become willing to allow His hands to shape us.

The *First Fruits Series* walks us through the lifelong cycle from the first step of seeking God's will all the way to the harvest season. It comprises multiple books to meet us wherever we are along the path.

- *The Door to Fruitfulness* is for those desiring to produce more for the Lord, but finding themselves inundated with unproductive busyness and unable to find a starting point. It is a map to the door of the Master Gardener's vineyard.

- *Beyond the Open Door* is for those who have actively crossed over into the Lord's vineyard and entered a place of God's vision for their life. It teaches how to lean on Him and see the world through His eyes.
- *The Seed Sower* is for those ready to go deeper and harvest more. It reveals how to produce fruit by sowing into the lives of others.
- *Seeds of Recovery* is a special training program that encourages participants to reach beyond themselves to embrace the needs of others. It deals with addiction issues and uses compassion and service for others as a method of recovery.

If you find your lips whispering the sweet prayer of surrender, "Lord, use me as You see fit", but need inspiration to step forward or desire comfort while waiting for His leading, the *First Fruit Series* is for you. It meets you where you are in your walk with Christ and encourages you for the journey of fruit bearing ahead.

The Seed Sower
(Coming Fall 2013)

Do you have a strong desire to harvest First Fruits for Christ and see more fruitful results in your Christian life? Then, it is time to start sowing seeds!

To have a beautiful garden ready for harvest in the summer, you must be willing to plant many seeds in the spring. The same concept is true of our Christian walk. Embark on this forty-day challenge to be a seed sower. As you sow a different seed each day into the lives of others, you will marvel how this seemingly small act creates great change in your own life and in those lives around you.

Seeds of Recovery
(Coming Fall 2013)

Seeds of Recovery is a special culinary and agricultural training program dealing with addiction issues, while providing a certificate program for use in a culinary-related career. The training also includes a series on the farm-to-table, local food movement and how it affects health and nutrition. The emotional and spiritual portions of the training encourage character development, professionalism, and the use of compassion and service for others as a method of recovery. *Seeds of Recovery* motivates participants to reach beyond themselves to embrace the needs of others.

Tammy L. Jordan

Notes

www.ingramcontent.com/pod-product-compliance
Lightning Source LLC
Chambersburg PA
CBHW030236100526
44584CB00015BB/1522